Return to the Great Mother

ALSO BY ISA GUCCIARDI, PH.D.

Coming to Peace

The Four Immeasurables: Meditations

Return to the Great Mother

Isa Gucciardi, Ph.D.

Edited by Laura Chandler

Red Cow Publishing
San Francisco

RED COW PUBLISHING

Red Cow Publishing, San Francisco, CA

redcowpublishing.com

Printed in the United States of America

ISBN-10: 0989855406
ISBN-13: 978-0-9898554-0-2

Note to the reader: This book is intended as an informational guide. It is not a substitute for professional medical care or treatment.

Cover designed by Catherine Marick

Cover photo by Deborah Hall

I Can Feel You by Laura Chandler, Copyright © Lulu Bucket Music 2005

This book is dedicated to the Earth

I can feel you trying to be born
I can feel you like a storm
Little twister making a fuss
Rising up from the dust

I can feel you inside of me
Tossing and turning endlessly
We don't know just what's begun
We won't know until it's done

I can feel you like some fate
All that pushing still you're late
You're just yearning to be free
Still not sure what you'll be

In the blinking of an eye
First we're born and then we die

I can feel you trying to be born
I can feel you like a storm
Little twister making a fuss
Rising up from the dust

Rising up from the dust . . .

- Laura Chandler, *I Can Feel You*

CONTENTS

CONTENTS

ACKNOWLEDGMENTS

Many people offered their support in the writing of this book. I would like to thank Laura for her insight and skill; Cody and Catherine for their technical wizardry; and Simone for her tireless dedication to detail. Thanks also to Alexis, Catherine, Joanna, Linda, Lindsey, Rachel, Sandra and Deborah for their invaluable contributions, and all of the women whose births and experiences of the Great Mother were documented in this book.

RETURN TO THE EARTH

Childbirth changed me. It brought me close to death and showed me life. I met myself in a way I had not known before. The experience of childbirth introduced me to a vital source of power that led me through the experience of giving birth that countless women across time and geographical space have gone through. Yet, I had not understood before that giving birth was an initiation. I'd never known that there would be a deep resource of power within me, that I could draw upon and could channel, that would help me navigate giving birth. I am not unique. I believe every woman can access this resource. However, it has become more difficult to do; in part, because of the loss of connection to our own natural rhythms, which comes from a larger separation from the earth. I wrote this book to help women restore their bond with this source of power. This book offers news ways of relating to birth and experiencing the birth process. It also contains numerous contemporary cases of people who have benefited from drawing upon this resource, and offers a tool that will assist you in doing the same.

As our experience of the world becomes more mediated by technology, it seems that our connection to the earth lessens. In many ways, people have lost touch with the priorities of nature and this creates an imbalance within us. We no longer know where or how our food is grown. We often do not know where the source of our drinking water lies. Many people spend their days working in artificially lit environments without access to fresh air. When we relax, it is often with television, video games, mobile devices, and other forms of entertainment that can take us away from our own natural rhythms.

This separation from nature has a profound effect on our emotional, mental, physical, and spiritual wellbeing. Losing touch with nature in this way causes us to miss the power of significant moments in our lives, such as birth, death, puberty, the sexual encounter with the other, and, for women, menses and menopause. These are important initiatory events, events that challenge us to expand. Yet, even the idea of initiation in contemporary society seems foreign.

In most traditional cultures, rituals and ceremonies have evolved around initiatory events. Rituals are created to channel the power that is released as one form of being dies and a new one is born in a particular way.[1] The process of giving birth is one of the most important initiations any woman undergoes. When she is disconnected from her biology or when she has not cultivated a relationship with herself that embraces her biological processes, serious problems can arise. At a minimum, she may be ill prepared to meet the physical, mental, emotional, and spiritual demands that giving birth requires. As a result, the power of the initiation of her birthing process will be lost to her.

Medical science has become the primary vehicle women rely on to navigate birth. While providing important assistance when it is needed on a physical level, the medical realm does not offer women many other resources in terms of emotional, mental, or spiritual support as they approach giving birth. In traditional societies, healers who assisted in the physical processes of birth were often the same people who played a role in maintaining the spiritual health of the society. In cultures where shamanic practices are found, for instance, the same shaman plays the role of doctor, minister, and counselor.[2]

Over the last forty years, there has been an increasing number of birth support providers, such as doulas, midwives, counselors,

---

[1] Mircea Eliade, *Shamanism: Archaic Techniques of Ecstasy*, trans. Willard R. Trask (Princeton: Princeton University Press: 1964).

[2] Eliade, *Shamanism*.

acupuncturists, chiropractors, hypnotherapists, and massage therapists, who specialize in working with pregnant women. Prenatal yoga classes are growing in popularity and can be found in cities and suburbs throughout the world. As women begin to recognize the significance of birth, not just as a medical procedure, but as an initiatory event with important implications for their own personal development, women can take back the power of birth that belongs to them and channel it into greater connection with their own evolution, the evolution of their children, and the healing of the planet through the creation of a more conscious society.

THE GREAT FEMININE

The concept of a Great Feminine principle is common to many cultural and religious traditions. The icon of the Great Feminine is viewed in these traditions as the generator and caretaker of life. The images of the Great Feminine vary from tradition to tradition, but the values and qualities of these images are surprisingly consistent. Whatever her form, she is always considered a protector and guardian of life.

Images of mother goddesses predominate in many archaeological finds from Ancient Egypt. The forms of the Great Mother in Egypt include those of animals seen as good mothers, including the lioness, cow, and hippopotamus. In ancient Greece, many sanctuaries and temples were dedicated to the embodiment of the Great Feminine that took the form of goddesses such as Hera and Gaia. Gaia is considered to be a very ancient goddess who personifies the Earth in a variety of forms.

In many cultures, the Great Mother principle is viewed as a force that encourages fertility and protects against disaster. In the Andean culture, the goddess Pachamama personifies this principle. In spiritual traditions in the Himalaya, the female deity Tara has a variety of aspects. Each aspect is considered to be an embodiment of different elements of compassionate assistance. Similarly, Quan Yin is a female deity revered throughout China and Southeast Asia. Her followers call upon her for assistance and deliverance from adversity.

In Catholicism, the Virgin Mary is considered to be the mother of God. In the Hopi tradition of North America, Mother Earth and the Corn Mother are believed to be the mothers of all living things. In the Hopi tradition, as in many others, the concepts of the Great Mother are closely tied with the powers of the Earth – the life-giving waters, the sun, the night sky. This understanding arises from the recognition of the ways in which women's bodies are in synch with the rhythms of the earth.

For instance, a woman's menstrual cycle is very close to the cycle of change exhibited by the moon through its phases, 29.5 days. As the moon progresses from the new moon, to the waxing moon of increasing light, to the full moon, and to the waning moon of decreasing light, so does a woman's estrous cycle build and wane.

The Mayans correlated one of their calendars related to the rhythms of the sun's waxing and waning influence over the seasons to the human female's gestation period. This may have been because the Mayans understood that a woman's body is constantly engaged with the dance of birth and death from month to month and this engagement naturally aligns women with the larger processes of birth and death that are mediated by the Earth.

Contemporary Western women have largely forgotten the intimate connection their bodies have with the cycles of nature. This is because the focus of their lives often takes them away from it. In a similar way, women have been separated from concepts of the divine feminine in spiritual pursuits. This separation has occurred over time and comes in part from the loss of connection with the Earth and the domination of masculine forms of divinity that populate Western traditions of spirituality.

THE MEDICALIZATION OF BIRTH

The emphasis on the patriarchy in spiritual affairs is mirrored in cultural affairs. This is particularly true in medicine, where women constitute only a small percentage of doctors. While the number of female doctors has increased in recent years in the U.S., they still total only 30 percent. This percentage remains disturbingly low.[3]

The roots of this trend can be traced back to Europe, in the Middle Ages, when male barber surgeons began monopolizing the birthing process, which had formerly been mediated by female midwives. During this time, women who provided birth support were labeled witches and were exiled, punished, or even burned at the stake.[4] By the 1700s in England, the Anglican church fathers were in charge of issuing licenses to those who were permitted to attend births. It should be noted that the predominant view of the pain of labor held by these church fathers was that women were being punished with labor pains because of original sin attributed to the biblical Eve.[5] The bias against women persisted in the English colonies, where the licensing boards assigned with granting licenses to midwives were made up of male government bureaucrats rather

---

[3] Gianna Fote, "Women in Medicine: How Female Doctors Have Changed the Face of Medicine," *Yale Journal of Medicine and Law* 8, no. 2 (2012), accessed May 27, 2013, http://www.yalemedlaw.com.
[4] Barbara Ehrenreich and Deirdre English, *Witches, Midwives, & Nurses: A History of Women Healers* (New York: Feminist Press, 1973).
[5] Ehrenreich and English, *Witches.*

than male clergy. This practice continued, and births attended by midwives licensed in this way were the norm until the 1900s.[6]

By the early 1900s, it became clear that birth was a business, and many leaders in the medical community began to solidify this fact by instituting policies that would ensure that women see only doctors in hospitals, abandoning midwives and homebirths. The campaign against the age-old profession of midwifery was in full swing by 1915, with influential doctors like Joseph DeLee leading the pack. In a widely published text by Dr. DeLee, he states that birth is a pathological process that requires intervention by medical doctors.[7] By 1930, the American Board of Obstetrics and Gynecology had been established. The Board lobbied Congress to exclude non-members from attending births, which meant midwives would be excluded. More generally, it meant that women would be unlikely to attend births, since most medical schools only admitted men. This helped set the course for the medicalization of birth in the U.S., which increased exponentially at this time.[8]

The medicalization of birth has continued to increase, with 37 percent of births occurring in hospitals in 1937 and an increase to 99 percent of births occurring in hospitals in 2010.[9] By 2010, Cesarean births had increased to 32.8 percent of all births in U.S. hospitals.[10] This is more than double the (15 percent) rate the World Health Organization recommends that Cesarean births not exceed.[11] In spite

---

[6] Ehrenreich and English, *Witches.*

[7] For more information on DeLee, see for instance, Judith Walzer Leavitt, PhD, "Joseph B. DeLee and the Practice of Preventive Obstetrics," *American Journal of Public Health* 78, no. 10 (1988): 1353-1361, accessed May 27, 2013, http://www.ncbi.nlm.nih.gov/pmc/articles/PMC1349440/.

[8] Richard W. Wertz and Dorothy C. Wertz, *Lying-In: A History of Childbirth in America,* expanded ed. (New Haven: Yale University Press, 1989).

[9] Wertz and Wertz, *Lying-In*; and Centers for Disease Control and Prevention, National Center for Health Statistics, "VitalStats," accessed June 10, 2013, http://www.cdc.gov/nchs/vitalstats.htm.

[10] "Births – Methods of Delivery," Centers for Disease Control and Prevention FastStats, Accessed June 10, 2013, http://www.cdc.gov/nchs/fastats/delivery.htm.

[11] World Health Organization, *Monitoring Emergency Obstetric Care: A Handbook* (Geneva: World Health Organization Press, 2009), p. 25,

of the increased medicalization of birth, or perhaps because of it, the United States, one of the richest countries in the world, ranks 51st worldwide for infant mortality, a disturbing fact.[12]

In recent years, inroads have been made to reduce the medicalization of birth. This includes training programs for midwives, the establishment of birth centers that provide an option "in-between" home birth and hospital birth, and an increase of ten percent in home births between 1980 and 2009. Certainly, science and medicine are important adjuncts to the birthing process. Many women's lives have been saved by modern medical procedures when they have encountered insurmountable obstacles when giving birth. However, the tools of medicine should not supersede the birthing process itself. They serve the process best when used in moderation and with great consideration, not as a matter of course.

In her book *Pushed*, Jennifer Block gives an excellent example of the way our culture has come to regard medical interventions as the norm, rather than the exception, for birth, and how the intervention process is not necessarily the better choice for mothers and their babies.[13] In the wake of Hurricane Charley, Heartland Medical Center, a hospital in Port Charlotte, Florida, lost power for nearly one week in August of 2004. This necessarily forced the hospital to step away from standard hospital procedures during the time of the power outage. Under these circumstances, births in the hospital largely went without drugs or medical intervention and returned to the natural rhythms of the birthing process.

---

accessed June 10, 2013,
http://whqlibdoc.who.int/publications/2009/9789241547734_eng.pdf.
[12] Central Intelligence Agency, "The World Fact Book," accessed June 10, 2013, https://www.cia.gov/library/publications/the-world-factbook/rankorder/2091rank.html. Note that the CIA rankings are from highest to lowest infant mortality, and the United States is 174 on their list of 224 countries and locations. So, there are 50 countries and locations whose infant mortality rate is lower than that of the U.S.
[13] Jennifer Block, *Pushed: The Painful Truth About Childbirth and Modern Maternity Care* (Cambridge, MA: Da Capo Press, 2007). The example that follows was reported by Block.

Specifically, all inductions were cancelled and Pitocin, a drug given to induce labor, was not administered. Epidurals were not administered. Doctors did not break a birthing mother's water to speed up the birth process and mothers were sent home unless they were in active labor. Notably, almost no Cesarean sections were performed.

Normally, all of these procedures at this hospital (and hospitals around the country) are routine. Epidurals are given for pain. Pitocin is given and waters are broken to induce labor. Cesarean sections are commonly recommended not only when the life of the baby and mother are at risk, but also when labor is simply taking longer than is common, or thought to be common.

The results of this unexpected experiment were impressive. As a consequence of this shift away from the standardized medicalization of the birth process, fetal distress and interventions after birth dropped to almost zero during this time period. Even first-time mothers had quick and relatively easy labors. Most interestingly, the births that occurred at Heartland Medical Center during the time without power were more evenly distributed between day and night, as compared to the usual concentration of births at the hospital, which occur during "working hours" (Monday to Friday, 9 a.m. - 5 p.m.).

There are no easy answers for how to change medicalized birth so that the health care system and its providers are able to offer even more support to mothers and children by attuning to the natural rhythms of birth. Yet, it is an important question to raise and consider. At the very least, it is essential that we begin to recognize that giving birth is not simply another medical procedure like setting a bone or removing an appendix. It must necessarily be regarded as part of something much larger and with far reaching implications.

BIRTH AND THE PROCESS OF INITIATION

Giving birth is one of a series of important initiations a woman may experience in her lifetime. Initiations are intimately tied with change. They bring the initiate from one state of being into a new state of being. Initiations accomplish this task by putting the initiate through a series of experiences that challenge them in a particular way and bring them into new ways of being and of understanding. The initiate must meet these challenges and overcome any obstacles in order for the initiation to succeed in bringing about these changes.

Today, many people going through initiations and many people managing initiations do not have a clear understanding of the nature of the power and vulnerability that is at the heart of initiation. Initiates must render themselves vulnerable to initiatory processes in order for initiations to become complete, and the power in that vulnerability must be managed carefully and thoughtfully. Most importantly, for an initiation to be successful, that power and vulnerability must be safeguarded and dedicated to the initiate.

The process of meeting an obstacle and overcoming it in order to ultimately gain greater insight and power is described by Joseph Campbell as the "hero's journey." The "hero's journey" is an initiatory experience. Every woman takes this journey when she gives birth and it can be the primary initiation a woman undergoes in the course of her life.

Often a woman encounters herself in an entirely new way during the process of giving birth. She may encounter the effect of traumas long buried, or she may encounter fear long denied. She may also discover power deep within herself that she had never imagined.

When the processes of birth are allowed to take their course, a woman with the proper care has the opportunity to come to terms with whatever may arise. In doing so, she may experience a shift into a new way of being or understanding. Yet, when the birth process is interrupted, or not properly held, the power of the initiation is often lost or distorted.

MANAGING INITIATION

In traditional cultures, the way a culture meets and manages the initiatory processes of its individual members is one of its defining qualities. The management of these initiations is generally accomplished by helping the initiate move through a ritual of some kind. Initiatory rituals can be very elaborate and well defined. In fact, anthropologists generally learn about a culture through the study of initiation rituals.

Rituals and culturally defined structures are good management tools to direct and hold the power of the initiatory process. However, a significant drawback to many rituals and cultural structures is that they have been designed to direct the power that is released in the initiatory process into the society's structures, rather than dedicating it to the initiate. When the power of the ritual is channeled into societal structures, cultural norms are solidified and carried forward from one generation to the next.

When the power of an initiatory process is directed into societal structures, it tends to make the culture and society stronger and the individual identity of the initiate weaker. This process binds the individual to the structures of the society in which the individual lives and ensures the continuation of those structures. Because the individual identity of the initiate is weakened in this process, initiation rituals can act as a deterrent to individualized expression in these cultural contexts.

For instance, puberty rites for young women in virtually every culture are very clear: The power that is released as the old forms of girlhood fall away and as the new forms of womanhood emerge does not belong to the female. The rituals around female puberty in many traditional cultures transfer the power of this initiation from one male to another, usually from father to husband.

Weddings, in Western culture, still manage this transfer of a woman's power from male to male. The question, "Who presents this woman in marriage?" has historically been answered by the father, as he literally hands his daughter over to her husband. The power of biology that rests within females is almost never allowed to stay with the female, either in traditional or modern cultures, as she moves from one initiatory process to another.

Traditionally, when women have sought to claim this power for their own, they have been exiled or punished. This was demonstrated in the witch trials of midwives in the Middle Ages in Europe. These women sought to keep the power of birthing women with birthing women. They did not want to dedicate that power to the patriarchal cultural structures; and they paid a price for seeking to dedicate the power of the most important initiation a woman passes through to the woman herself.

In traditional cultures, this redirection of the power of initiation into societal structures was in many ways a necessary part of the continued existence of the culture. In particular, it maintained the group-oriented mindset. This mindset was at the very heart of the survival of cultures that relied on adherence to social structures to keep them safe and to ensure the continuance of the tribe. Today, however, many societies are more individualistic and the needs of these societies and their members are different. This is why it is so important to seek a new understanding of and engagement with ritual and the power of initiation and to redirect that power towards the individual. When the individual is empowered, the society will be empowered, and both will evolve.

STEPS ON THE PATH OF INITIATION

Biology largely dictates the initiations that women experience. The emotional, spiritual, and mental changes that accompany women's biological changes are profound, even if they are not always understood or explored. To better understand these initiatory experiences, it is important to consider how they correspond to a woman's reproductive cycle.

The Initiatory Stages of the Female Reproductive Cycle

1). Birth: This initiation represents the first experience of the world as an individual being.

2). Puberty: This initiation begins the shift from childhood to womanhood.

3). Menses: This initiation occurs each month as a woman's body changes form when her uterus builds and sloughs its lining. The biological change is evident, but she also undergoes a complex and poorly understood emotional change.

4). The sexual encounter with the other: This initiation involves the shift that occurs when a woman's focus moves from herself to the other.

5). Giving birth: In this initiation, a woman further expands her focus from herself to the other and necessarily redefines herself to include the needs of another.

6). Menopause: This initiation involves how a woman redefines herself as she loses the capacity to bear children. In many traditional societies, women past menopause have a completely different status than women of childbearing age.

7). Death: Only a few initiations in a woman's life lie outside her reproductive processes, and these revolve around death.

RECLAIMING THE POWER OF INITIATION

In his important work, *Beyond the Brain*, Stanislav Grof suggests that the way a woman experiences her own birth is a template for the way she will approach giving birth in the future.[14] Further, a woman's experience of her own birth defines and articulates her spiritual path and the way subsequent initiations are met. In this way, her earlier initiations inform and can even dictate the outcome of her later initiations. Interrupting the birth process and subsequent spiritual initiation processes of women giving birth is potentially harmful and can have long-lasting consequences.

In modern births, the power of the initiation of birth is often co-opted by doctors, pharmaceutical companies, insurance companies, and hospitals. It is also co-opted by the fear of pain and the influence of friends and family. It is difficult for women to hold onto the power of the initiation of birth under these circumstances. The unfortunate implication here is that the subsequent initiations of women interrupted in this way will be affected by their inability to hold onto the power of their birthing process.

Based on the level of interruption of the birth initiation caused by unnecessary interventions in the birthing process today, it seems reasonable to suggest that many women experience incomplete initiations when giving birth. This can lead to spiritual crises that are

---

[14] Stanislav Grof, *Beyond the Brain: Birth, Death and Transcendence in Psychotherapy* (Albany: State University of New York Press, 1985).

not understood. For example, some women may feel a level of powerlessness they cannot explain.

Because women (and men) have lost touch with the process of birth, women have no idea that they are engaged in a spiritual path driven by their biology. They also have no idea that they are moving through one initiation process into another as they experience their own birth, puberty, monthly menses, and the sexual encounter with the other. Finally, they have no idea that the ways they have met these earlier initiations influence the way they are likely to meet the initiation of giving birth.

The lack of information and resources regarding the importance of viewing birth as an initiation does not affect birthing women alone. It also inhibits the ability of caregivers, such as ministers, teachers, doctors, and other birth professionals who are charged with guiding women through birth, to provide deeper levels of support. Also, the partners of birthing women are uninformed about the larger initiatory processes that are occurring, so they miss out on their own deeper initiatory experience of birth.

In recent decades, midwives and other birth professionals have been working to create a dialogue about reclaiming the birth process. One of the early innovators of the modern midwifery movement is Ina May Gaskin. In 1971, she and her husband established one of the first non-hospital birthing centers in the U.S., based in Lewis County, Tennessee. The Farm Midwifery Center, which is still active today, emphasizes the spiritual significance of birth, and recognizes the importance of family and friends being able to be present at the birth. Throughout her long career, Gaskin has received many awards, has written several influential books, is credited with introducing the Gaskin Maneuver for relieving shoulder dystocia, and has taught workshops throughout the world.

The American Journal of Public Health published a study that focused on the outcomes of 1707 women who received care from midwives of The Farm in Tennessee between 1971 and 1989. These births were compared to outcomes of over 14,000 physician-attended hospital births in 1980. It concluded, "Based on rates of perinatal death, of low five-minute Apgar scores, of a composite index of labor complications, and of use of assisted delivery, the results suggest that, under certain circumstances, home births attended by lay midwives can be accomplished as safely as, and with less intervention than, physician-attended hospital deliveries."[15]

Since the start of the modern midwifery movement there has been some advancement, with the establishment of birth centers outside of hospital settings and the creation of more homelike environments within hospitals. The conversation is still one-sided much of the time, however. Medicalization remains the dominant paradigm in the birth process. The good news is that this conversation has involved more and more women and birthing professionals who are waking up to the possibilities of bringing the conversation back to the basics of birthing, be it at home or in the hospital.

[15] Mark A. Durand, MD, MPH, "The Safety of Home Birth: The Farm Study," *American Journal of Public Health* 82, No 3 (1992): 450-452, accessed May 27, 2013, http://ajph.aphapublications.org/doi/pdf/10.2105/AJPH.82.3.450.

MEETING THE GREAT MOTHER

The birth alternatives Gaskin was advocating in the 1970s quickly spread throughout progressive communities in the U.S. and abroad. In the late seventies, I was part of an alternative spiritual community in the Berkshire Mountains of Massachusetts and joined a group of young mothers who helped each other in their birthing processes using many of the principles Gaskin was advocating. Most of us gave birth at home, but some of us chose the hospital setting. We supported each other during the birthing process and afterwards.

It was in this setting, during my own birthing process, that I first encountered the Great Mother. My first birth had been very difficult. Both my child and I had come close to dying. As my second birth gained momentum, I began having flashbacks to the trauma of my first birth. As I was losing ground in maintaining my stability, I became aware of a bright, luminescent, mirage-like presence. It was generating and exuding a huge amount of power. I felt that power flowing into me from above and to my left.

I stabilized with this influx of power and could feel the warmth of the embrace of it. I identified it as a tremendous female presence. It identified itself to me as the Great Mother. I stayed focused on that presence for the rest of what was to be another very difficult birth. Again, both my child and I skirted the edges of danger.

The labor lasted over 24 hours, yet I did not take my focus off of the Great Mother. She held my focus and my heart and I was able to walk down the same path I had walked in my first birth, returning from the threshold of death a second time. As I walked that path in my second birth, I recognized the place where the Great Mother had held me in my first birth, the place where everyone thought I would die.

I am sure I would have never had the fortitude to sustain myself, or my child, in either birth without the help of this benevolent presence. Afterwards, in all the births where I helped other mothers, I found the Great Mother there, guiding and helping in just the ways that were needed for each individual birth. In some intense situations, I could feel the Great Mother sustaining the lives of those mothers and children in the same way she had sustained mine.

As my children grew, I became less connected with the birthing community. I thought we had changed birthing for good with all the work we had done in those spiritual communities in the seventies. After I went back to school and started developing the therapeutic model of Depth Hypnosis,[16] I became aware of the crisis that still existed in the birthing realms through my students and clients. It was surprising to find women and birthing professionals struggling with the same issues we had struggled with so long ago.

One of the most disturbing aspects of this ongoing struggle around birth was the lack of support that birthing professionals were experiencing. I could see they were throwing their own life energy into the void that was created as birthing mothers lost power, giving birth under conditions that were not always supportive. As I reentered the conversation around birthing, I realized that birth professionals and women giving birth needed more tools to support them. So, I worked to develop them.

---

[16] Depth Hypnosis is a model for self-transformation that incorporates Buddhist understandings regarding the nature of the mind, shamanic understandings regarding the correction of imbalance, techniques from hypnotherapy, and transpersonal psychology.

WORKING WITH THE GREAT MOTHER

The simplest and most immediately helpful tool I have developed for those working with birthing women is the Great Mother Meditation, which is included in this book. The simplicity of this meditation allows women to encounter the Great Mother on their own terms. A woman does not have to hold any set of religious beliefs or obey any culturally defined rules to encounter this power. She may perceive the Great Mother in any form that has meaning to her.

As women connect with this powerful, vital force, they are able to invoke the Great Mother at the time of their child's birth. In this way, they regain access to the ability to safeguard the power of the initiatory process of birth. This is a service that the Great Mother has always provided in any cultural context in which she is found. The calling in of a power of some kind to guide the initiate and hold power throughout the initiation is common to most initiation rituals. The Great Mother meditation is designed to help those who use it to connect with a power that will assist them during the initiation of birth.

In many traditional cultures, the power of the Great Mother was invoked to guide and rule birth. In ancient Japan, Tamayorihime, the Mother Goddess, was known to be implicitly present to guide and rule the birthing processes. Her role was celebrated through Shinto rituals. In ancient Greece, Hera, the Mother Goddess, presided and ruled over all births and assisted women in labor. Ajysyt, the Great Mother of the Yakut people of Siberia, was said to be present at every birth. She ruled and facilitated birth and she brought the soul of the child.[17]

In the Great Mother meditation, it is the Great Mother who guides the initiation of birth. The form the Great Mother takes and the way she is experienced varies from individual to individual. This is because the power she brings is unique to the needs of each person encountering her. For instance, one woman giving birth may experience her as soft and loving, while another may experience her as fierce and driving. One woman may see her as a fairy, while another sees her as a bear. Whatever the experience, it is understood that the experience of the Great Mother and the power and teachings that she brings are meant to assist the woman giving birth in the place where she needs it most.

I created the Great Mother meditation based on my work with visualization therapies, traditional hypnosis, Depth Hypnosis, and certain shamanic principles. It is important to remember that this is a non-dogmatic process. There is no right or wrong way to do it. It does not require that someone working with this meditation believe in a power called the Great Mother, or believe in a higher power at all. It simply requires a willingness to set aside judgment and give it a try. If the meditation is helpful, it does not matter whether it is a way to contact an ancient power called the Great Mother or just an exercise in imagination.

The Great Mother meditation is similar to a hypnotic induction. When working with it, the pregnant woman is guided into an altered state of consciousness by someone she trusts, preferably someone who has worked with the Great Mother in this way before. However, it is also possible for a caregiver who has not worked in this way before to lead the induction; or, in some cases, the woman giving birth will not have assistance, so she will need to connect with the Great Mother on her own.

For each of these scenarios, it is helpful if a woman works with the meditation before her actual birth, developing a connection to

[17] *Encyclopedia Mythica Online* s.v. "Ajysyt," accessed March 13, 2013, http://www.pantheon.org/articles/a/ajysyt.html.

her guide, the Great Mother. She can do this alone or with assistance. Ideally, women who encounter the Great Mother through this meditation will connect with her again and again during pregnancy for guidance and nourishment. However, some women will encounter her for the first time during the birth itself.

CASE STUDIES

As you will see in the following case studies, women who return to the Great Mother during their pregnancies and child rearing years find tremendous support and guidance. The Great Mother is considered to be ever present during the initiation process. Even those women who have no spiritual practice at all benefit from the encounter with the Great Mother at crucial moments in their birthing process. Each woman's experience of the Great Mother is different. Yet, the presence and support that the Great Mother offers remains consistent. Whether a mother finds herself in a medicalized birth, a homebirth, or somewhere in between, she can seek the assistance of this non-dogmatic form of power to help guide her.

The following case studies are drawn from my students. They are all Depth Hypnosis Practitioners and have learned methods for working with the Great Mother through my classes. All are accomplished professionals from a variety of backgrounds who work with women in various stages of the birth experience. The names of the women in the case studies have been changed to protect their privacy. Each of the Practitioners who submitted case studies has also included a synopsis of her experience of and personal work with the Great Mother. I am deeply appreciative of their contributions to this book and their dedication to this work.

JOANNA ADLER
Depth Hypnosis Practitioner, Psychotherapist, Mother
Marin County, CA

I was first introduced to the concept of the Great Mother in a class at the Foundation of the Sacred Stream. I was not sure exactly what to expect, although I had an idea that the archetype or energy of the Great Mother had something to do with nature, and the power of creation. I did not know that what I was getting into would change the course of my life. Over the last years of working with her, the Great Mother has taught me how to be in the world in a way I didn't really know existed.

My experience of the Great Mother is that she is a source of great sustenance, love, support, growth, creativity, and fierce compassion all rolled up in one big package. She has taught me how to truly be of support to my clients as a clinical psychologist and Depth Hypnosis Practitioner. Also, she has taught me how to mother from a place that supports me, as well as my kids. The Great Mother has also taught me about the ebb and flow of life: the creation and dissolution of all that is, from the smallest insect to the largest universe, and everything in between. Her support has been invaluable to me in my work, in my mothering, and in my humble attempts to understand the nature of existence.

Since meeting the Great Mother, the work I do in the world has become an attempt to bring the power and support of the Great Mother to others. Many of the clients that come to me are in some stage of becoming a parent. They are struggling with infertility, or feel unbalanced in pregnancy or awash in the trials of the postpartum period. Others come to me for help in aligning themselves in order to traverse the initiation of childbirth, or to recover from a labor and birth that were traumatic, or for support in grieving the loss of a pregnancy or baby. Sometimes my clients are just trying to figure out how to parent.

Whatever the case, in my experience, the energy of the Great Mother is healing, supportive, guiding, and unconditionally loving. I access this field myself as I sit with my clients, and I guide others to access her wisdom as well. With her support, it seems it is possible to move through any trial and find healing.

GREAT POWER

My first encounter with the Great Mother was in a guided meditation in the *Initiations of the Sacred Feminine* class at Foundation of the Sacred Stream:

I ask to meet the Great Mother. I am standing in an open place. A great wind/energy blows towards and around and over and under me. I feel very afraid of this power. It is huge, and full of light and sound and torrential movement. I am close to being knocked over.

My good friend/guide stands behind me. He braces me and helps me to move forward towards the source of this energy. With him, I find my courage. It takes Herculean effort to move forward into the streaming wind/movement. I lean in, and I move forward slowly.

Finally I am able to jump into the center, the source of the wind. The Great Mother appears in white. She says, "You have passed the test. You are now to be my handmaiden." She is beyond good and evil. She is more powerful than all; she encompasses all. She is the creative force and ground of being. She takes me to her garden and we sit and have tea.

To me, this encounter epitomizes many others I have had, and witnessed others having, with the Great Mother. At times it seems paradoxical. She is a huge power, yet gentle at the same time.

Over the last years of working with the Great Mother, she has taught me many things. She has shown me how to hold my power, and how to be a container or vessel through which power can run to support others. She has shown me how scorn and shame can tear my container, as well as how collapsing in the face of judgment can close off the flow of available power.

I have learned that when I sit in the flow of this creative, loving force, the degenerative forces of blame and shame and collapse can simply be washed away down the stream. Each time I sit in the field, I am taught how to hold more power, and I am shown the patterns I no longer need.

The backdrop of the Great Mother has also highlighted the places where I haven't opened to my own needs. She has lit the places inside me that I had deemed too raw or unacceptable or ugly for others to see, and, thus, had disowned as well. She has taught me how to take care of those parts of myself, and with each part cared for, I have felt more whole, and less ruled by negativity in the shadows.

RESPECTING THE CONNECTION TO THE GREAT MOTHER

A pregnant woman, Mary, came to me for support in preparing for her labor. I guided her through the Great Mother Meditation:

The Great Mother appears as a monolithic female Buddha. She is made of stone. She is a symbol, a door to a greater energy, and the energy coming through. I am told this is a good place for me to sit each day. I am not to think here. There is a transfer of energy behind and inside the statue. It is connected to me.

My instruction is to respect the connection, in order to be in the right place to have this child. The Great Mother has no boundary. She is like a big ball, giving birth to herself. She is in a constant state of giving birth again and again. The transition to motherhood from here is not so shocking, it is already happening all the time. It is effortless and all connected.

There is a big ceremony coming. I am to give myself over while not being completely surrendered.

There is a baby boy. He needs my physical energy to be ready. He is very joyful, and not worried. He has a plan. I am shown we have done this together before. I must not have resistance.

I must not think about or judge what is happening. The Great Mother is showing me the people that will be involved in the birth. I am to thank them for participating, and to create a psychic birth plan with them. I am to get ready mentally. Then, I am to let go and be restful.

Mary is shown the labor to come as a "ceremony" to which she is to give herself over. She is also shown that, as she aligns with the force and flow of the Great Mother, her transition through labor can be effortless and connected.

EXPERIENCE

Leila was worried she was not up to going through labor and delivery. She stated that she didn't know how she would get through it. In a Depth Hypnosis session, she was guided through the Great Mother meditation:

I am moving up the knoll of a hill. There is a temple behind me. It is grassy all around. The temple is fuzzy. The temple turns into a brown bear on a wooden structure. The brown bear is the Great Mother. She is safe and powerful. I feel calm, protected. She roars. I can access her power. It is the birth energy. I know how to move it through my body.

The conscious experience of knowing how to move the birth energy through her body changed Leila's approach to her labor. At the next session, she reported feeling more prepared and more relaxed.

CONNECTION

Another pregnant mother, Kristin, came to me three weeks before her due date wanting to feel more connected to her baby.

I am standing by a mountain. There is water running, and grass. It is sunshiny. Beautiful. Calm and warm. I am met by a butterfly. She is the Great Mother, carefree and innocent. She shows me the spirit of my son. He is heavy, and more serious. I am to sit and stay with him. Being with him doesn't feel natural. I feel oppositional to this.

Discovering this hidden opposition to her child opened the door for Kristin to do the deeper work that was needed for her to be able to welcome her son into her family.

TRUST

Shaylene was pregnant and came to see me struggling with what it would be like to be a mother. Her own mother had been an alcoholic, and my client had learned early on that her mother was not trustworthy. She realized that she felt mothers in general were not trustworthy. This is her experience with the Great Mother meditation, as she explored the issue of trust:

The Great Mother says to be patient and not to worry. Trust I will learn how to do things. Use people around me. Don't forget I'm not alone. Trusting. This is my big learning. I can look to the baby for signals about what she needs. Trust and faith are where I am to focus. It is my path. Doubt and fear bring me to my child self where I am small and disappointed. I could not talk with my mother. She wasn't really there. I sit with the Great Mother and this child part of myself. She needs a mom who is sober and present, and who will talk with her. She needs a mom who will be curious about her. As she sits with the Great Mother, I feel my child self is healing.

PRESENCE

Josephine experienced intense anxiety before and during her pregnancy. Her mother had also struggled with anxiety. We did the Great Mother meditation:

I am in a garden. There are tons of flowers. There is a white fence, and a white house. There is an older woman. She is an energy, an angel, a woman. She tends to the garden. She is the mother I never had. She is grounded and supportive. She says, "I'm here for you." She has such a wise energy. I always hoped someone would be like this with me. All my unsettled places are no big deal for her. She can be there and be grounded, without judgment or feeling uncomfortable.

This is a good example of how sitting in the field or energy of the Great Mother can settle difficult emotions.

PLAY

Robin became unexpectedly pregnant with her second child at ten months postpartum. She wanted to find a way to welcome this child, even though she felt anxious, fearful, and tight in relationship to the pregnancy. This is her experience with the Great Mother meditation:

I see green. There are walls and a wood floor. There are two windows. I am in a tree house. I can see branches outside the windows. I feel safe. There is a breeze. I sense it is the Great Mother.

There is a giggling, and a quiet rustling of the breeze in the trees. It is the Great Mother. She is overwhelming — open and free. I want to breathe her in. Refreshing. My heart and gut don't feel constricted any more. I feel full of energy. I can jump and dance. This is an anger-free, frustration-free place.

I want to show my son this place. I can play here. Whatever I need, I can just take a deep breath in. The windows don't close. I always have access to her. Even from inside I can still hear her. When I breathe, I picture leaves rustling in my lungs. I don't feel the constriction now. I haven't felt a presence like this in a long time.

LOSS

The following series of meditations are highlights from sessions that took place over two years. Angelica went through a series of four *in vitro* fertilization (IVF) treatments. During this first meditation, she is 16 weeks pregnant with a pregnancy that she will soon miscarry, and she is feeling disconnected from the baby:

The Great Mother shines a light on me. It is a window into my baby. The baby is bigger, squirmy, and moving around. Exploring its home. The Great mother says, "The hurt is necessary, and we will both get through it." I am to remember, whatever happens, that I am moving towards the feeling of holding my baby in my arms.

Although it was not clear at the time what was happening, in retrospect the Great Mother was steadying Angelica for her loss.

REBIRTH

After the miscarriage, Angelica felt judgmental towards herself, and blamed herself for the loss. This is her next encounter with the Great Mother in a Depth Hypnosis session:

The Great Mother wraps me in a love blanket. She wants me to feel love, from the heart, towards myself. It feels green…new…living. I can be the source of that. I have felt cold and dead inside. I do have the strength to do these things. I can be powerful and strong and shine this light. It's worth it, even if it is just for me.

Her contact with the Great Mother helps her begin to move out of blame and judgment and into love and kindness towards herself.

NOURISHMENT

Approximately three months later, she is in the middle of an IVF cycle:

The Great Mother is the sun. She is shining rays of light and there are nutrients pouring into me. She has laid a bed in my womb. I feel full and supple and maternal. I am told I am a part of this field of life. I am not outside looking in. I feel many flickers around. They are spirits wanting to come in and be born.

Although this particular IVF cycle did not result in a pregnancy, Angelica reported feeling at peace with the outcome.

FEAR

Three months later, another embryo has just been transferred into her womb. This is the session that follows:

The Great Mother is holding me, and I hold my womb with my loving heart and my strong belly. I gave the strength in me I had to give. I'm connected to the whole life force, and I have that to share and show other beings how to plug in to it.

I show them by humming, and having faith in my intention. I shine the light from my heart and give them (the embryos) faith and intention. They want to be part of it, my heart.

My only obstacle is my fear of the things I have no control over. This grip of fear looks like something that can keep these lives from growing. The fear can cut me off from the warmth of love I send them.

The Great Mother says, "See fear for what it is. Be compassionate towards it." This is less scary. The fear is now more like a friend who has been hurt. I can again hum and shine my light.

This session highlights the Great Mother's teachings on the power of compassion. Angelica is shown how her fear can get in the way of sending her nourishing love/life force to the embryos floating in her womb. She is also shown how to antidote her fear with compassion.

This transfer, again, does not produce a pregnancy.

OPENING

Several months later, another embryo has been transferred into Angelica. Again she connects to the Great Mother in her Depth Hypnosis session:

The Great Mother and other guides walk me up a hill to a very old place. There are rocks around. We go up to the top of the hill. There is a pool there. I sit. They want me to drop my hopes and wish for a baby into the pool. I see it resting there safe, and cared for by the guides. There is mutual care happening. It is full of meaning. I feel complete. There are lots of other pools. I'm not at the center. I am to trust that wherever I end up, it is a place where I can be. I am letting go. Opening.

Angelica was taught to hold her wish as if it were already fulfilled. She was taught to trust that, no matter what happens, she is okay. Also, it is important to note that she was shown that her "pool" is not the only one. This visual was an antidote to her feeling of being singled out in having to endure this difficult journey with so many pregnancy attempts and losses.

This IVF cycle finally resulted in a viable pregnancy with twins.

ACCEPTANCE

This is her Depth Hypnosis session at thirty-three weeks of pregnancy:

The Great Mother says to let go of my tightness. All is okay. All three of us are okay. I am to let go of the struggle against discomfort, and not being able to sleep. I am to accept the rest I get. I am to let go of the struggle. It's quieter. I am to work with the Great Mother in labor. She will help with fear of the unknown and fear of pain. I am to let her hold my hand and open to the scary place.

Angelica had been having trouble sleeping, and was fearful she would lose her babies. She was also afraid of the pain of labor. The Great Mother showed her how to hold these difficult feelings in a way that was healing and she ultimately gave birth to two healthy babies. Angelica later reported many times how important her work with the Great Mother had been in traversing her difficulties becoming a mother.

LINDSEY FITZGIBBONS
Depth Hypnosis Practitioner, Mother
San Francisco, CA

My first experience of the Great Mother was when Joanna Adler came to the prenatal yoga teacher training I was attending. She led the group in the meditation to meet the Great Mother. I was seven months pregnant at the time and fell asleep. When the group shared after the meditation, many participants told amazing stories of what they saw and experienced. I wanted another try, so I began doing Depth Hypnosis sessions with Joanna to prepare for my upcoming birth. I did a handful of Depth Hypnosis sessions with her before the birth, working with the power of the Great Mother.

SUSTENANCE

When my birth arrived, it took 36 hours of labor to wear out my resistance and finally let the Great Mother in! And she came. What I didn't know at the time was that the Great Mother had merged with me and helped me birth my son.

I had never felt so powerful in my whole life. I had been exhausted, ready to give up and go to the hospital. (I had a planned homebirth.) Yet, when I finally let the Great Mother in, my water broke and labor took off. I was able to stay with the contractions more fully and had a surge of energy. I gave birth to a beautiful baby boy with her help.

In my first labor, I didn't understand my relationship to the Great Mother as well as I did in my second labor. My second labor and birth were remarkably different from the first, as I had spent the intervening two and a half years working with and developing a relationship with the Great Mother.

During my second pregnancy, I spent many hours with the Great Mother, asking her to help me through what was a very difficult pregnancy. She showed me a field of energy that provided everything I needed to nourish and take care of myself.

It's hard to put my experience of the Great Mother into words. It is an all-encompassing, bountiful, generative, supportive energy whose giving is unending. She is the Earth and all that the Earth has to offer. Knowing that I can connect to something so profound and nourishing and wise by simply turning my attention to her has really changed my life. I've felt more connected to myself, to nature, and to the universe, which is something I've lacked as I've gotten older and spent less time in nature.

The Great Mother is one of my most trusted guides. She is with me when I do any journeywork for myself and with my clients. I connect with the Great Mother daily, but specifically when I'm having a difficult moment with my kids, when I'm sick, and when I feel unsafe. She has taught me to sit and be present with what is, how to better care for others, and myself, and how to protect myself when someone is being aggressive. She's also teaching me how to connect to her field of energy when I feel under attack instead of engaging in negativity.

After my work with Joanna, I decided to take the Depth Hypnosis Practitioner training at the Foundation of the Sacred Stream. I now work as a Depth Hypnosis Practitioner and some of my clients are pregnant and some are preparing for birth. I've used the Great Mother meditation with clients and I am always moved by the way they experience the Great Mother.

I've seen how connecting with the Great Mother allows women to listen more to their inner wisdom. There are so many voices around them as they prepare for birth, and spending time with the Great Mother creates space for them to listen and take care of themselves.

RELEASE

One of my clients, Anita, wanted to go back to the moment of her own birth before she gave birth herself. She did this through a prenatal regression within a Depth Hypnosis session. It was immensely helpful for her to understand the dynamics of what was going on at the time of her birth so she could understand her role in giving birth.

This is Anita's experience with the Great Mother in the prenatal regression:

The Great Mother takes me to the room where I was born. I see it was full of my mother's burdens. It is difficult, but I am able to lean into the Great Mother and get the support I need. Although it is difficult to be with them, when I see the burdens in this way, I can see they are not mine. They belong to my mother.

I see myself being born. As I am being born, half of the burdens in the room go away. I feel heaviness in my chest. I want to both avoid and release my connection with these burdens. The Great Mother comes, and I feel my breath full and easy as she brings warmth and light into the room and bathes me in it. It feels like the Great Mother is repatterning my connection to my mother's burdens.

Anita said that seeing her birth allowed her "not to buy the story of the burdens" her mother always told her she would experience in one form or another. It helped her understand that she could give birth without the sense of being burdened in the way her mother had been.

ALEXIS COHEN
Depth Hypnosis Practitioner, Artist, Doula
San Francisco, CA

I was introduced to the idea of the Divine Feminine in my early 20s and became very interested in goddesses. The archetype of a strong, loving, compassionate, and kind woman was like a cold drink of water for me.

Through my studies at the Foundation of the Sacred Stream, the concept of the Great Mother became very tangible to me. I found I was able to connect directly to her power through meditation and the shamanic journey. This direct connection with the power of the Great Mother continues to inform me in my life.

A key concept for me is trust. In my personal work, I continue to open and soften to the Great Mother and to life. To trust the Great Mother, I have to take the time to step into my true nature. I have to remember that I don't need to hide anymore. It is quite a practice because I come up against the places in me that are in reaction to past trauma, the places where I don't feel safe. My work is to allow the Great Mother to help me heal and integrate these alienated parts of me and become more whole.

I see the Great Mother as a guide both inside and outside of me. When I tune into her, she is always there and she is everywhere. She is pure creative potential flowing through all of life. She is nature and she is within me.

In my Depth Hypnosis practice, it is my intention to help women and their partners connect with the power of the Great Mother before they enter into the birthing process. During the course of supporting a woman in labor, I am actively and constantly checking and strengthening my connection to the Great Mother. I work to expand and relax into the field of the Great Mother during a birth, and this is very helpful and supportive for the laboring woman. I also help to remind her about the Great Mother and the way that she had originally connected to her power. If she has a particular image that she relates to the Great Mother, I may gently remind the laboring woman to connect with that image. This is especially true if she is having a more challenging time during labor.

Learning about and coming into more direct contact with the concept of the Great Mother has completely changed my life. I feel as though my life is dedicated to serving the power of the Great Mother and to being aligned with the flow of life and nature that she represents. I feel her flow in my life and body, and I pay attention to how she points to any obstructions to the flow. She helps me understand the places where the flow is interrupted, and she helps me know where to bring support and healing.

I am happiest and most at ease when I am aware of my connection with the Great Mother and in communication with her. At these times I expand into the breath of life. When I feel a lack of connection with the Great Mother, I feel lethargic, unhappy, and contracted. I am coming to understand that even when I am contracted and having a hard time connecting with the Great Mother, she is there. I know I am being supported even when I am in the uncomfortable place of contraction.

I try to bring this same understanding to the women I help in my doula practice.

ANCIENT WISDOM

From the first moment I met Lisa, she had a sense of calm about her. Whenever we talked about birth, a serene knowing smile would stretch across her face. She prepared for her birth by attending classes and she had a solid partnership with her husband.

She had also worked for the Peace Corps in Africa and had witnessed several births. I guided her through the meditation to the Great Mother at our last meeting together before her birth. The Great Mother appeared to her as a wise, ancient African woman.

It was a sweet rainy San Francisco day when Lisa went into labor. The sound of the raindrops outside was present as she rested in between her powerful surges. Her labor progressed smoothly. After about an hour, the surges become stronger and more frequent. It seemed as though it was a good time to go to the hospital.

Her birth was very quiet. She was internally focused. Her husband and I "held space" for her. When we transferred to the hospital, the staff was very respectful of her process. She was standing in her personal power in a strong way. The birth was serene. She was immoveable in her focus. After a couple of hours of pushing, her baby arrived. Lisa's all knowing smile was intact as she kissed the top of her baby's head.

At the postnatal visit a few weeks later, I asked Lisa about her internal experience of her labor. She said quite simply that the entire time she was in labor she was following the steady, knowing, and ancient feet of the Great Mother down a flight of clay stairs. Those stairs led her to her baby.

FLOW

Ana had a little scare at week 27 of her pregnancy. She was having frequent surges and she was beginning to efface and dilate. She had to go to the hospital and go on some medication to slow down the process. She was put on bed rest for ten weeks.

We had our last prenatal meeting at around 37 weeks. She had met with her doctor the day before. Her doctor had told her that she did not have to be on bed rest any longer. In our Depth Hypnosis session together, we talked about recognizing the way that energy flows toward birth. I told her that sometimes when women are put on bed rest, there can be a slowing or freezing of that flow. When I mentioned this to her, a look of recognition came across her face. She knew what I was talking about.

I led her and her husband in the Great Mother meditation. When doing the Great Mother meditation as a couple, one person holds the image or field of the Great Mother as the other partner shares how he or she perceives the Great Mother. Everyone perceives the Great Mother in his or her own way and everyone has his or her own experience.

Ana envisioned a meadow that was very beautiful and covered in ice and snow. Independently, her husband also ended up in a meadow; but, in his vision, it was a beautiful spring day. He felt the sun very strongly on his face.

When Ana spoke, she asked the Great Mother for a healing. As the healing progressed, she saw all the snow and ice in the meadow melting. At the end of the healing, she was standing in the same meadow as her husband, with the sun on her face.

After the meditation, she reported that she felt like she had released a lot of the tension from the weeks of bed rest. They both felt very close after having shared a very similar vision.

I got a call from them a few hours after I had guided them through this meditation. Soon after that meditation, Ana went into labor and had her baby not too long afterwards. Her baby was born in the caul. This means the baby is born in the amniotic sac. This is a very rare event and it is seen by many cultures as an auspicious beginning for the baby.

CALLING POWER

Cindy had a very prolonged pushing stage in her labor. The doctors were starting to get concerned about the baby's heart rate. It wasn't an emergency yet, but the baby's heartbeat was definitely taking longer to recover.

What was so striking about this birth is that I kept feeling as though there was a nurse behind me. Several times I turned around to speak to the nurse and no one was there. I just kept getting the sense of a very loving and nurturing angelic woman behind me. I realized that I was feeling the presence of the power of the Great Mother assisting me.

When it became clear to Cindy that her baby needed to be born, she started to chant, "Nature Mama, come on Mama" over and over again as a way to connect with the power of the Great Mother. She needed this chanting in order to birth her baby. The power came in and through her. She gathered this power and she pushed her baby out.

It was absolutely astounding to see the shift in the progression of the labor once she started chanting and calling for the power of the Great Mother.

OVERCOMING FEAR

Jenny had a history of panic attacks. She came to me for help with her anxiety and her panic. She had been anxious about her birth, and her anxiety increased when she learned the doctors wanted to induce her labor.

I had guided her through the Great Mother meditation, and she had a very powerful vision of the face of the Great Mother.

When I arrived at the birth, I expected her to be very anxious. Yet, when I walked into the labor room, she was very calm.

When she sensed I was in the room, she opened her eyes. As the next surge started, she said. "Every time I have a surge, I see the face of the Great Mother. I haven't told anyone that yet because I think they will think I am nuts." She then had a surge.

Her labor continued for hours, and she was calm and focused. At one point she began to feel very scared and asked for medication to ease the pain, even though she had wanted to have a natural childbirth.

Because I knew that a natural childbirth had been her goal, I led her back to her breath and suggested that she connect with the Great Mother. I kept bringing her back into the connection with the Great Mother's face that she had experienced in the first meditation to the Great Mother as she started to get scared. Each time, I reminded her to connect to the face of the Great Mother and each time she pulled out of her fear as she made that connection. This went on for hours.

Finally, her baby was born without the panic attack she feared, and she was able to have the natural birth she wanted.

DREAMING THE GREAT MOTHER

I guided Ashley and Jon, a wonderful expectant couple, through the Great Mother meditation. They both already had a very strong meditation practice. The night after I had introduced them to the meditation on the Great Mother, Jon had a dream of the Great Mother.

She came to him as a very strong and loving wise older woman. She told him that the birth would be hard but that everything would be okay and that Ashley could do it.

The birth was lovely. They had done a lot of work of setting the space with calm lighting, devotional music. They had created an altar. The labor was going well, and then Ashley began to lose steam. She started doubting herself.

We gave her a lot of reassurance. It did not seem to be helping. Then Jon said, "Remember my dream and what the Great Mother said. It's hard but she knows you can do it." This reminder helped Ashley greatly. This message was very powerful for her and it filled her with endurance and confidence. It was as if her whole body remembered the dream and responded with renewed vigor. In a very short time, their baby was born.

ADVICE FROM THE GREAT MOTHER

Lola had been laboring for close to 48 hours during her home birth. It was clear from the surge pattern of her contractions that the baby was in a unique position. This position was potentially contributing to a longer labor.

Lola was getting tired, so I suggested that she get into the tub so she could relax. I knew this would be a good place for her to reconnect with the Great Mother through a facilitated meditation.

She connected with the Great Mother while she was relaxing in the tub. As she meditated with her, the Great Mother reminded her that she had scoliosis. The scoliosis was contributing to the issue with the baby's position. She suggested that instead of curling around the baby during labor, Lola should be more upright to give the baby more space. The Great Mother suggested that I help to support her in being upright.

So I got behind her while she was sitting and gently aligned her shoulders, and pulled her back a little. We did this for a short while. Everything changed. Lola moved into active labor. She had her baby several hours later.

I never would have connected the issue with the baby's position to scoliosis, and I was very grateful for the Great Mother's guidance.

LISTENING

Eve had been in labor for three days. We were at home for most of the time. When we did eventually go to the hospital, she labored in a room that had a birthing tub. Because of the long opening and thinning stage of the labor, Eve was exhausted. When it came time for her to push, she didn't feel she had enough strength to push.

I suggested that she take a break and try again once she had had a good rest. The doctors were being very conservative and didn't want her to wait for the delivery of the baby. They didn't like how long the labor was taking even though the baby seemed fine. The doctors finally suggested a Cesarean. Eve was very upset.

This was one of those moments where a choice had to be made between the natural pacing of the mother and baby and what the hospital staff wanted. This can be a hard place to navigate. I suggested that Eve get in the tub so I could help her connect to the Great Mother through guided meditation. She was able to relax and connect with the Great Mother. The Great Mother came to her as an image of a large woman as big as nature with outstretched loving arms. The Great Mother told her that she and the baby just needed more time.

As she was in the tub and connecting with the Great Mother, she got a lot of good rest. Her strength began coming back to her and the forces within her began to get stronger. She was able to move through the rest of the birth at her own pace in a powerful way.

Her healthy baby was born naturally. She had listened to the Great Mother and she had made a choice that was right for her, in spite of all the pressure from the hospital staff to do something different.

WEB OF LIGHT

Chloe labored in her home for several days. At around 3 a.m. on the third morning, she announced that she wanted to go to the hospital.

She realized that she was having trouble letting go at home because she felt scared. Several years earlier she had had heart surgery. She wanted to be at the hospital to have her heart better monitored. Although she was still in early labor, we went to the hospital so she could feel safe and supported.

When we got to the hospital, she was checked to see how fully she had dilated. She was about four centimeters. She was checked several hours later and she was still at that same point of dilation. At this point, the doctors suggested augmenting her labor with medication if her dilation did not increase within a few hours.

The doctors left the labor room. Her husband decided to take a nap.

Chloe had described herself as "not spiritual" so I didn't want to introduce the concept of the Great Mother. Yet, I connected with the Great Mother in meditation as I was sitting behind her. She was sitting on a yoga ball and she was resting her head on the bed. In my meditation, I saw a beautiful and supportive energetic web of light around Chloe. It was in an egg-like shape around her body.

I saw the egg expand and then I heard, "This is seven centimeters." I realized the Great Mother was showing me energetically what being opened to seven centimeters is like for a woman during labor. So I helped focus this information toward Chloe as I stayed focused on the Great Mother.

Chloe shifted her position a bit, and I realized she was receiving this information as she rested. Her labor shifted, and it seemed that she had opened to the Great Mother's instruction without realizing that was what she was doing.

As her labor progressed, she continued to dilate. The doctors came in a bit later and checked Chloe. She was seven centimeters, and there was no more talk of giving her medication to increase her labor. This was an astonishing and confirming experience for me. I understood the power of the Great Mother in a new way.

GREAT MOTHER!

Melissa had been laboring well at her homebirth. When the baby's head crowned, it did not continue coming forward. Instead, it was crowning for about 30 minutes, which is a very long time for this stage of labor. Melissa was quite tired, as she had been laboring for a long time.

The baby's heartbeat started to decelerate. The baby had to be born. Melissa began pushing with all of her might. The midwife started to feel as though it was becoming an urgent situation and expressed this to Melissa. She said, "Okay, if you don't push the baby out with this push I am going to have to cut an episiotomy."

I reminded Melissa about the Great Mother. I said, "Call on the strength of the Great Mother." The midwives heard me, and, spontaneously, we all started calling on the power and strength of the Great Mother. We were suddenly all chanting together, "Great Mother! Great Mother!"

The power of the Great Mother could tangibly be felt in the room. It was almost as though a stream of energy flowed in from the chanting. Melissa pushed one more time, and the baby's head was born with that push.

She did not need an episiotomy. She did not even tear as the baby was born.

LINDA GRUBER
M.S. Traditional Chinese Medicine, Acupuncturist, Herbalist,
Doula
Mill Valley, CA

I first became aware of the concept of the Great Mother through classes I took with Isa Gucciardi. I work mainly with women and couples who are trying to conceive a child. I also work with women during pregnancy, birth, and in the postpartum period.

I experience the Great Mother as a powerful "field" that is beneath us all. This field is deep and rich and supportive. My experience of the energy of this field is that it emerges upward to envelop us in love, strength, and our own innate power and wisdom.

When I learned about the concept of the Great Mother, I began focusing on allowing the process for each person to happen, rather than feeling like I had to "make it happen." This was a huge change for me. It helped me feel I was not responsible for other people's experience and it helped me step away from my perfectionism when perfectionism wasn't necessary.

Of course, I was still very caring and compassionate in my service to my patients. The Great Mother just made it possible for me to take a step back. At the same time, I learned I could hold the space for my patients, knowing that everything would happen in its own right time. This was very helpful because things don't always happen in the time my patients or I would like. I work with the Great Mother daily in my practice. I invite her into my office and ask her to work with me for the highest and best outcome for patients I see each day.

EAST MEETS WEST

I started working with Amy in 2009. Our work together has been a journey of learning for us both. She came to see me because she wanted to get pregnant. She had stopped taking birth control pills a year before and her period had never returned. She was afraid of needles, but she had several friends who had worked with me and who had become pregnant. So she was willing to give it a try even though she remained skeptical.

In her first session, we just talked about acupuncture. In our second session, I was able to use three needles. We had to count them as we put them in and we had to count them as we took them out. As we worked together, Amy opened more and more to her healing journey. This journey resulted in the birth of her son and daughter. She had twins and she was elated to be their mom.

Since Amy had such trepidation of needles, we did a great deal of visualization work. I worked by calling the power of the Great Mother into my sessions with her. The office was filled with the essence of the Great Mother as we worked. I talked to Amy about the Great Mother meditation and one day she was ready to do it. She connected with a strong powerful guide almost immediately. She named this guide "Abby."

Amy began working with Abby daily. Abby became her most trusted guide. As she worked with Abby, Amy became more and more connected to her own power and clarity. As this occurred, she made choices that best suited her fertility journey. In the end, Amy used a combination of Eastern medicine and Western medical treatments to become pregnant.

She received an intrauterine insemination and she received it in a conscious way. She asked the Great Mother to accompany her on the path the insemination would create for her. Even before she received the results, she knew she was pregnant. She also knew she would be having twins and that they were a boy and a girl. At this point, she had worked with guidance and the Great Mother so closely that she could trust her knowing.

Once her pregnancy was confirmed, she had some anxiety and fear. We worked together to ask the Great Mother to protect the babies' spirits. As Amy worked with her in this way, she became more and more clear about what each baby needed. Amy perceived that each one was protected in its own "sack" by their own guidance and the Great Mother.

Amy received acupuncture and journeyed to the Great Mother throughout her pregnancy. Toward the end of her pregnancy, it seemed as though the babies were ready to be born. She started having preterm labor. We did more acupuncture and we journeyed to the Great Mother. Amy also created art to solidify her connection with these two beings. The labor stopped, and then at 35 weeks and six days, the babies were ready to be born.

A FIRST

At their birth, I called on the power of the Great Mother to bring ease and grace to everyone. I asked the Great Mother to guide and protect this birth, and she did. We did acupuncture and visualization throughout the labor. During the entire day of labor no one came into the room to interrupt us, even though we were in a hospital.

When Amy's dilation was at 10 centimeters, Amy was feeling "done" and exhausted. The doctor on call was a perinatologist. He was used to high-risk emergency births that usually involved Cesarean sections. The doctor ordered an epidural, because it was twins. Also, he wanted her to have the drug just in case she had to go to surgery.

Labor slowed down, as it often does after an epidural, and Amy was able to rest a bit. Then, an hour later, under the watchful eye of her doctor, Amy birthed Jack, an adorable, healthy baby boy. Fifteen minutes later, out came Hazel, a happy, healthy baby girl.

Amy and her husband were filled with love and gratitude to see their babies. I was grateful to the power of the Great Mother. She, I believe, allowed the doctor to let the birth happen naturally.

Interestingly, the doctor, who had been in practice for years, had never attended a vaginal birth of twins.

SANDRA LLOYD
Depth Hypnosis Practitioner, Doula, Mother
San Francisco, CA

I have been working as a doula assisting women in birth for many years. Since meeting the Great Mother as part of a workshop I took with Isa Gucciardi (*Tracking Spirit in the Birth Environment*). I have been consistently working with the Great Mother at births. I am humbled by the way the Great Mother brings her strength and wisdom to me as I offer my care and support to birthing women. I always connect with the power of the Great Mother before I join a birthing woman in labor, and ask for her protection and guidance.

In many circumstances, I have witnessed the Great Mother's power as it affected the behavior of care providers in hospitals. Sometimes, the change in behavior has been evident when doctors, midwives, or nurses have suddenly demonstrated dramatic shifts in their usual ways of practicing and interacting with birthing women.

The effect of this power has also been made evident in the way that a practitioner, whose negativity might be affecting the birthing woman's experience, has simply left the room. Over and over, I have seen birthing women experiencing the power and support of the Great Mother in ways unique to them.

In my first experience with the Great Mother, she appeared to me as the Corn Mother with a large group of corn maidens that filled a huge field. At every birth since that time, the Corn Mother and her maidens have opened the path to the birth portal. More recently, the Great Mother came to me in tripartite form: The Corn Mother, A

Native American woman chief, and a white marble Quan Yin. It was the first time she had appeared in this way, and the first time I had seen her face. It was ancient.

She came to me in this form when I asked her to be present for the birth of a mother named Meredith. This was a challenging labor, beginning with a medical induction. The process of this birth shows the power of the Great Mother in ways I have often experienced as a doula.

THE LONG WAIT

Meredith was admitted to the hospital in the evening in order for the doctors to induce her labor. There was a serious medical issue, cholestasis, which is a malfunction of the mother's gallbladder. This occurred more than two weeks before the baby's "guess date." This birth mother sought doula support for her labor, but was not intent on having a natural birth. Nor was she interested in doing any Depth Hypnosis or journeywork before her labor started.

Friday, 7 p.m.: Meredith was excited, but apprehensive about birthing her baby before she might be ready to be born. It was very challenging for her to stay calm and she worried about the birth going well. She was worried about medical intervention and her own health.

I helped calm her by helping her pay attention to her breath and then by playing relaxing music as she settled in for sleep. She was given medication to help soften and ripen her cervix and encourage labor to begin. At the start of the induction, her cervix was three centimeters dilated, barely effaced, and the baby was high in her pelvis.

Saturday morning, 9 a.m.: There were no changes in Meredith's cervix overnight and she was given another dose of the cervical ripening agent. Her husband brought her flowers and breakfast from her favorite restaurant. Early labor surges started in the afternoon and she was relaxed playing monopoly to distract herself. She seemed to forget she was having a baby.

By evening, the surges had slowed and we were considering what the next step would be. Meredith had one of many difficult spells. She felt she wasn't ready to have her baby. She was full of fear and she started to "over think" everything. We spent time focusing on relaxation with hypnotic suggestions. I reminded her to give attention to her purpose for being in the hospital – to birth her beautiful girl!

Saturday night, 7 p.m.: For the rest of the evening and most of the next day, Meredith was engaged in all the processes that come into play with a medical induction. She was afraid of the strength of the sensations that Pitocin, the drug that is given to start contractions, might create. We talked about "welcoming and embracing the sensations of labor" as well as the chemistry involved in moving labor forward.

At night she rested, because she felt fatigued and was not experiencing the labor as we had hoped. Her baby was mostly in a very "sleepy," nonreactive mode, as evidenced by her heart rate. Throughout the night, Meredith inhaled oxygen to enhance her baby's wellbeing.

We all had been hopeful that this induction would go smoothly and swiftly. Yet, as often happens when a pregnant woman and her baby are being asked to birth before either of them are ready, the induction can last for days. It becomes a waiting game.

Sunday morning, 9 a.m.: Meredith was upset. She said she felt "like a patient" and said she hated being a patient. She had another difficult spell. She said she felt disconnected from her body because the labor was not progressing, even with all the medical manipulations. She was upset that she was still stuck in a tiny room in the hospital.

We decided to walk and she spent some time rhythmically rocking back and forth in a rocking chair. This was to help Meredith feel more engaged and connected to her body and baby again.

By early evening, she had received the maximum amount of Pitocin that can safely be administered. Mild surges were occurring every three to five minutes. Meredith barely felt them. There was still no active labor.

The doctors turned off the Pitocin and we regrouped. She was four centimeters dilated and her cervix was 50 percent effaced. The baby was still high in her pelvis, as one would expect of a baby that is weeks before her "guess date."

Sunday evening, 6 p.m.: It had been 48 hours since we started the induction. The plan for the night was to rest again, to take a dose of the cervical ripening agent, and see if labor could get started again. Meredith was discouraged.

I suggested that it might be the moment for her to consider the benefits of connecting with the Great Mother. After all that she had been through, she was finally willing to entertain the possibility that this connection might be of help to her.

I guided her through the Great Mother meditation. This is the report of her journey:

I arrive at a clearing in a forest. There are lots of small animals. I am alone here. It is very peaceful. I feel safe and captivated by the beauty of this place.

I see a path, and at the end of the path in the distance is a shining sun that seems to be calling me closer. I move along the path toward this bright light but I don't feel compelled to reach it.

I ask if this is the Great Mother and receive the answer, "yes." The Great Mother says that she will guide and protect me in my labor and in the birthing of my baby, as well as in the days and weeks ahead.

I then ask her for guidance for the labor, and she tells me: "It is the journey that is important, to pay attention to the lessons and be present in the journey all along the way."

It can be very challenging for a mother when her labor is medically managed, as Meredith's had been. After this journey, she felt more hopeful and happy. She was glad to feel this connection to the Great Mother.

Monday morning, 9 a.m.: Meredith reported that nothing had happened during the night. She was feeling sad. She was upset because the labor induction process had been going on for days and she was not yet in clear labor. She was afraid that the induction would fail and she would have a Cesarean birth.

The doctor and midwife suggested "breaking" the bag of waters and starting the Pitocin drip again to prompt labor. We discussed the benefits of keeping the bag of waters intact at this early point in labor and Meredith decided to refuse that procedure.

With suggestion hypnosis, Meredith's attention was redirected to welcoming the Pitocin, rather than resisting it, and to inviting her surges and their intensity, and to encourage her body to shift into labor. Again, the Pitocin drip was started at the lowest level.

What happened next is what I consider to be one of the surprise miracles of this labor. In the morning, a new nurse came in to care for Meredith. I had never seen her before in the many times I had been at this hospital as a doula. She was completely present for Meredith. She fully acknowledged Meredith's experience and spoke with love and compassion.

It was as if an angel had walked into the room. She offered to do some energy healing work to support Meredith and her labor. Meredith, who had no prior experience with energy healing, and who was very discouraged, said, "Sure, I'm open to anything that will get this labor going."

Meredith's acupuncturist arrived, and I worked to strengthen and deepen my connection with the Great Mother. I directed healing energy to the mother and baby, and focused attention on opening the portal to birth for them. At the same time, her acupuncturist was connecting with the Great Mother and holding space for Meredith, as she had been all this time from another location.

Our nurse offered healing energy, holding her open hands above the reclined torso of the birthing mother. Meredith relaxed. The bag of waters released. Surges and contractions started occurring every two minutes. Meredith was in labor!

Her surges continued to be strong and frequent. The Pitocin was turned off. The baby was doing fine. After several hours of intensity, she began having doubts about her ability to keep the labor going. I suggested she go into the shower. As she showered, I offered suggestion hypnosis to help her move past doubt and to help her fully engage with her labor. I helped her with her breath, showing her how to breathe in deeply and release her breath deeply.

It was as if she was in a trance. Sometimes she dozed as the water rushed over her, and sometimes she swayed her body. Her husband and I were in the candlelit bathroom with her, directing the shower in rhythmic movements over her body. We alternately opened and closed the door of the shower to her commands of "Fresh air," and "Cold."

It was beautiful watching her labor.

Monday, 8:30 p.m.: As evening came, she moved to the rocking chair. Then back into the shower. Her surges were still coming strong at about one to three minutes apart. She said, "I feel like it's getting close." She was feeling a deeper connection to the work she and her baby were doing.

It was, however, going to be awhile until her baby was born.

As the evening wore on, Meredith began saying she could not go on. Our midwife came in to do a vaginal exam. It was wonderful news. Her cervix was seven centimeters and almost completely thinned out.

Still, Meredith was feeling like she couldn't keep laboring. So again, I helped her return to a relaxed state with hypnosis, and helped her focus on the work to be done. Over the next few hours, I observed her moving her hands with each surge much like conducting an orchestra.

Tuesday, 2:30 a.m.: Her surges definitely intensified. About an hour later, Meredith said she wanted an epidural. We discussed other options, but she was absolutely insistent.

Tuesday, 4 a.m.: We were all resting. Her cervix had not changed at all since 10 p.m. the night before. The uterine surges had lost intensity, so again we were back to the use of a low dose of Pitocin to support her surges.

We all reminded ourselves that our purpose here was to help this baby be born, and that we had to proceed the way we were because of her mother's medical issue.

Things were no longer flowing the way they were before Meredith insisted on taking the epidural.

Tuesday, 9 a.m.: Our midwife left. Meredith did not feel comfortable with the doctor who was now on duty. Her approach was completely "out of sync" with how the rest of the staff had been supporting Meredith. The doctor's negativity toward the situation was palpable. She had been on duty at the start of the labor on Friday, and Meredith had hoped she wouldn't need to interact with her again.

The good news was that Meredith's cervix was nine centimeters; however, the baby was still sitting pretty high in her pelvis. The surges had spaced out. There was a lot of talk about having few options left to help this baby be born. The doctor told us that the surges did not have enough force to bring the baby down and finish dilation. She felt the only solution was Cesarean birth.

After speaking with the doctor, Meredith started to feel like she wanted the surgery. I kept holding my attention on the Great Mother and focusing healing energy into the portal of birth.

Then, another small miracle happened. The nurse with the healing touch returned!

Tuesday, 11 a.m.: The acupuncturist and the helpful nurse and I gathered to focus on Meredith. We called the power of the Great Mother into the room. We asked for her guidance and repeated our ritual of healing from the previous day.

We kept directing bright, clear light onto mother and baby, while each of us focused on our own connection and relationship with the Great Mother. The acupuncturist was again connecting with the Great Mother and sending healing energy from a distance. I had a vision of the room and the bed held firmly by the earth, surrounded by rose crystals.

Tuesday, 12 p.m.: I decided to ask Meredith to get into a position that would help her baby descend. I positioned her on her side with her legs propped wide open. One leg was propped up on a table to assist the baby moving down.

I asked the Great Mother what else I could do to support this birth. The Great Mother told me to call the spirit of the baby. I was reminded that in spite of repeated suggestions over recent weeks to engage in positive, encouraging, and reassuring language with their baby, both parents had frequently chosen joking, negative, almost blaming language when speaking about their baby.

Now Meredith was thinking of her baby as being "difficult and stubborn." I was able to journey to the spirit of the baby. It appeared in the image of a baby porcupine. She was joyfully spinning and dancing and told me that she was indeed the spirit of the baby. I asked what was needed for baby to be born now. Without hesitation, she answered: "Respect" and "Protection."

I shared the information from this journey with the mother and father of the baby, and they both shrieked, "We LOVE porcupines!" They both had a lot of knowledge about the life and habits of porcupines and were delighted to know this about their baby.

Tuesday, 1:30 p.m.: The doctor returned to check in again and see if there was any change. Meredith's cervix was completely dilated and the baby had moved down some. We chose to wait and allow time for the baby to descend more. Meredith began talking to her baby, and she kept trying to relax into the relationship with the baby.

Tuesday, 3:30 p.m.: There had been no change in the baby's position. The doctors increased the dose of Pitocin. After discussion with the doctor, a plan was set to turn down the epidural and ask the mother to start pushing the baby out.

The doctor told her she was not optimistic about the baby coming out without a Cesarean procedure. Nevertheless, she instructed Meredith to try pushing with every bit of strength in order to birth her baby. Meredith told me that she felt the task of pushing sounded physically daunting. She said she just wanted to have a Cesarean birth.

I asked her what she had usually chosen to do when she was physically challenged. She responded, "I would take the easy way out." I suggested that this could be an opportunity to make a different choice.

In taking some time to reflect here, I again sought the Great Mother's support, because I was feeling some disappointment that Meredith might choose a Cesarean birth. The Great Mother told me: "You cannot learn someone else's lessons for them."

After resting a bit and feeling more sensation returning to her legs and bottom, Meredith asked her husband, the nurse, and me to help her start pushing. The nurse and her husband gave her lots of positive, gentle encouragement.

They started seeing the top of the baby's head.

Tuesday, 5 p.m.: Her doctor came in to check on the progress of the pushing. She told us that the baby was still in the same place in her pelvis and hadn't moved down at all. She said they were not seeing the baby's head, but just some swelling.

Again, this doctor had brought news that impacted Meredith negatively. Once again, the doctor had created interference in Meredith's efforts to birth her baby vaginally.

I began calling the Great Mother in all the forms she had revealed to me during this labor. I asked for help to find a way to move this mother and to move her baby into the right position to be born. I had a vision of the Ancient Native American Woman, the Corn Mother, and Quan Yin. The bright light of the sun was shining on the path of the birth.

With a little coaxing, Meredith was willing to regroup and try another way of pushing. I set up a squat bar and tied a sheet to it. Meredith propped her legs against the squat bar and could feel her body's urge to push. She grabbed onto the ends of the sheet and began to pull hard with each push. This was a perfect, natural position for her because she was a rower. She had a connection to this position from rowing and she was used to using the strength of her arms in this way.

Her baby started moving down the birth canal fast.

It wasn't long before we saw a lot of the baby's head. Our nurse called for a midwife because the baby was almost there. The midwife ran in as the baby's head was beginning to crown. Everyone was smiling.

I noticed that the doctor who had been so negative had quietly entered the room. She said she had just come to watch, that she wasn't needed for the delivery.

I was stunned. Her whole demeanor had softened and she was moved. She had come to witness this baby's arrival in this way – a way she had not trusted would work. It seemed to me that an important transformation was taking place with her as she joined us.

The midwife asked Meredith's husband to come near and get ready to help catch the baby. This was one of the most important things this couple wanted to happen at their baby's birth. He wanted to help catch the baby and lift her up to Meredith.

Tuesday, 6 p.m.: Meredith gave a few more pushes. The baby was born into her father's hands.

RACHEL YELLIN
Depth Hypnosis Practitioner, Childbirth Educator
Marin County, CA

I first began my work with women and birth as a doula and prenatal yoga teacher. That worked evolved into my teaching HypnoCentered Childbirth education classes and becoming a Depth Hypnosis Practitioner.

I teach more than 200 women and couples each year. As a Depth Hypnosis Practitioner, about 50 percent of my practice is working with women who are afraid to give birth, women who have had a traumatic birth, or women who are having a second or third baby and want to go deeper into what might be possible for them in the experience of birthing.

I was first introduced to the concept of the Great Mother through classes with Isa Gucciardi. It was something I had felt before at births and began working with directly as a result of Isa's classes. I experience the Great Mother as an energy or presence that holds exactly what a person needs while going through a major life transition.

When I was a doula, I would go into the birth room ready to defend the moms. This caused me to use up so much of my own strength and inner resources during births that I actually became ill. I developed severe adrenal fatigue, weight gain, and body pain. I drained every ounce of my own energy in order to give the birthing mother more energy. When the Great Mother came into my life, everything about the way I worked changed.

After learning about the Great Mother and how to work with her in a birth environment, I actually found that I had a reliable, caring, stable, strong support system to tap into, and this provided me with an endless supply of energy. It was at this time that I began to connect with the Great Mother before every yoga class, before every birthing class, and before any session where a woman was working on something birth related.

What became abundantly clear was that when I worked in relationship with the Great Mother, all the work that I did was a lot easier. I didn't have to know everything. I didn't have to have all the answers. My sense of patience and compassion increased enormously! The Great Mother even helped me develop tolerance for situations where I would have previously wanted to confront a medical care provider for doing something to a mother which I felt was totally unjust. Instead she provided me with a safe place to express all my feelings and get more clarity on the situation.

My life is greatly changed as a result of working with the Great Mother. Whenever I need something, the Great Mother is there like the best possible mother that ever could have existed. When I need strength, she is there. When I need to rest, she is there. When I need to express anger, she can hold it. When I need a compassionate kick in the pants, she is there for me. She loves me and that gives me what I need to manage whatever is arising. She also celebrates me. Like right now, I can sense her smiling and telling me how pleased she is that I'm going public like this about her!

Since I stopped working full time as a doula, I have only attended a handful of births with the Great Mother on my team. What I know for sure is that the Great Mother helped to keep the energy in each of those birth environments stable, calm, and grounded. She helped me to continually direct the power back to the birthing mother. My own connection with the Great Mother during births, regardless of whether the birthing mother was connecting with the Great Mother or not, kept me focused, relaxed, connected, and patient – way more than I'd previously experienced before working with the Great Mother.

A TALE OF TWO BIRTHS

Abby had hired me for the birth of her first baby. She wanted to have a natural birth. She took my birthing class, practiced prenatal yoga, and took good care of herself during her pregnancy. She did not have any concept of the Great Mother.

When Abby went into labor, she proceeded to have 48 hours with a baby whose position was causing a tremendous amount of back pain. She stayed positive, focused on her breathing, and did what she could to surrender into relaxation in the effort that the baby would rotate. However, after being exhausted and bordering on feelings of suffering, she decided it was time to go to the hospital to get an epidural. She was five centimeters dilated when we got to the hospital and as soon as she got an epidural, she was able to sleep. After a few hours, she was fully dilated and the baby had rotated to a position that facilitated an easier descent. Abby began to push.

As I watched her, I could see that she was acting like she was pushing, but in fact she wasn't. After two hours of "pushing," she turned to me and said, "I want to tell you something and I don't want you to say a word about it. I just want you to do what I tell you to do." I agreed to that. She said, "I'm done pushing and I want a Cesarean." My mouth started to open and she said, "No, seriously, you said you'd just do as I ask." I said to her, "Okay. I will go get the obstetrician and let her know of your wishes."

I left the room and told the OB the story. The OB said that she needed to assess the baby first, but if the mother wanted a surgical birth, that she is obligated to honor that request. The doctor went into the room and did a pelvic exam. She said, "You're baby is really low and his heart tones are good. I don't see any reason why you can't keep pushing." Abby said, "I'm done and I want the baby out. I want a Cesarean." So that's what happened. She had a normal Cesarean birth and a healthy boy.

Two years later, I got a call. It was Abby. She wanted me to be her doula again. I thought to myself, "Why?" She said she wanted to try to have a vaginal birth after Cesarean (VBAC) and she needed my help. I loved her and wanted to help her, so I explained that I'd be happy to be her doula again, but as part of the doula package, I offer a two-hour session of Depth Hypnosis. I explained what that involved and she said, "That's perfect. I really need to process what happened in the first birth."

When she came for the visit, she was ready to go deep. She was clearly very affected by her first birth and had some sadness and regrets about how it went. She recounted the details of the birth to me. She recounted the joy of going into labor. She recounted the connection with her baby. She recounted the back pain. She recounted the relief from sleeping. Then she got to the part about pushing. She hated the pushing. She hated everyone watching her. She hated the way she thought she looked and she hated the way it felt in her bottom. She hated feeling like she was going to poop all over the bed.

When I asked what part of the birth experience felt like it had the strongest reaction, she said it was all about the pushing. I asked her if we could do some trance work around that and she agreed. I told her we were going to start with connecting to an energy or presence that would help her understand or heal from the birth. I explained a little about the Great Mother, and she seemed very open to that.

I guided her through the Great Mother meditation. Here is her experience:

I feel safe. I'm in a redwood forest with soft pine needles, and speckled sun coming through. There is shade and it's cool. The trunks are big, the stream is bubbling through dark stones. There are a few butterflies. I come to a lake. There is a she-wolf sitting next to me. She is my companion. She is gray and white with rings around her eyes and big white paws. She has a pink tongue hanging out of her mouth and her eyes are blue/green. Her eyes are kind. She is fierce, yet compassionate. She has a lot of energy and strength, and she also knows how to go in the den and sleep. She will do anything for her babies. She will help give me a healthy baby. She tells me to let go of the mind, to be in the body. She tells me to start to train the mind to let go of the fear and pain and questions. She tells me to be in nature. She emphasizes the healing power of touch. She gives me a gentle lick and a hug. Her fur is soft and she is cuddly.

I asked her to ask the wolf if it would be okay to explore the experience of birthing her first child and to gather some understanding about the experience of pushing. Abby asked the Great Mother, who gave an enthusiastic and reassuring nod. I asked Abby to ask the Great Mother to go with her back to the birth. Abby told me she was afraid to go. I suggested she ask the Great Mother what to do about that fear. The Great Mother told her that she was just going to witness it; she was not going to re-experience it. This eased Abby's fear and she was willing to go.

In a trance state, eyes closed, Abby told me that the Great Mother was taking her further into the forest to find a safe place to be. She and the Great Mother sat down and she told the Great Mother what happened. She got to the part about pushing and recounted how much she hated it. She felt scared of the power in her body. She didn't want to make a mistake. She was afraid of the pain. She had the feeling that she had a protective inner tube around her lower belly. It was stuck. It was not fluid. It was immobile. There was a lot of stagnation. She said it was maybe digestive related, but there was definitely a feeling of being stuck.

Here is how the Depth Hypnosis session went:[18]

RY: So just allow yourself to concentrate on that stuck feeling in the bowels.

Abby: It feels like there is a fullness that has no outlet.

RY: As I count from three to one, allow yourself to go back to the situation, time, or place where you were first or most significantly having this same feeling.

Abby: I'm scared.

RY: Ask the Great Mother what to do.

Abby: She tells me to trust her and that she's coming with me. Everything is going to be okay. We are going to heal.

---

[18] This session uses age regression, which is one of the methods the Depth Hypnosis model incorporates.

RY: Three... Two... One...

Abby: I'm in elementary school. I'm six years old wearing jeans and a velour top. I'm working on rhyming and reading. It's really hard. I feel pressured. I am closed down and tightening. I am uncomfortable and I can't focus on the lesson. I look for an escape or I allow the distraction. I have to go to the bathroom. I have to go poop, but the bathroom is not clean and people are not clean and there isn't any good privacy in there. I am very uncomfortable. Everybody is looking at me. They know I have to go but I'm so embarrassed.

RY: So now, just imagine that your adult self could walk into that classroom and go see little Abby. How does your adult self feel toward little Abby?

Abby: I feel really sorry for her. She is so miserable and uncomfortable.

RY: And how does little Abby feel towards you?

Abby: She doesn't totally trust me at first, but then I point to the Great Mother to vouch for me. Little Abby really likes the wolf and believes the wolf that I'm good. So now I take little Abby and we leave the school through the playground and go into the forest. We walk over the stream and see chipmunks and animals in the forest and where they live. We go along and see all the different animals – the bears, the mountain lions, the marmots. We go through the forest and take little Abby home. We have a snack and she feels better. The wolf wants to help. The wolf starts to peel away all the stiffness around Abby' pelvis. She's peeling it off like old, discolored wood. There is a new skin that is revealed. The wolf is licking it and coating it in protection. The new skin needs time to heal and stay soft and open to this new sensation so the wood won't grow back. We are all learning a new way.

I help her finish this journey and she makes her way back. She sits up and says:

I had no idea that my life-long constipation problems came from holding in my poop at school after being so stressed in the classroom. My mother used to say that the bathrooms at school were kind of dirty and I should go at home if I could. Wow, the Great Mother sure did take care of that. I feel so bad for little Abby. She was so sweet and was doing her best and just felt totally judged and observed. I sure do wish she'd had the wolf with her when she was little. And man, do I wish the wolf had been with me when I gave birth. That sensation of pushing was exactly the same. The feeling of being embarrassed or not good enough; the feeling of being pressured. I just couldn't perform. I feel like the wolf really did a major repair job on me.

We concluded our session and I suggested that she talk to her new baby about the Great Mother and how she was going to assist with the birth. I encouraged her to turn to the Great Mother any time she has a concern or fear about birthing, and that she connect with the Great Mother when she needs support with parenting.

Abby liked all of this.

Six weeks later, I received a call from Abby's partner. He said that I should come fast because the labor was happening quickly. When I got to Abby's house, she was on her hands and knees in the entryway, breathing deeply and telling me the baby was coming. I looked at her bottom and could see that she was very tight, holding back, and struggling a bit with the amount of pressure.

I simply reminded her to call the Great Mother. Within moments, every part of her relaxed. She easily got in the car and pushed and breathed and pushed and relaxed for the twelve minute ride to the hospital. I called the hospital on the way and they met us with a gurney. We got into the birthing room, and a perfect baby was born about three minutes later.

Abby attributes her ability to give birth naturally after a prior Cesarean, in under three hours, to the support, guidance, healing, and power that the Great Mother provided.

CATHERINE MILLER
Depth Hypnosis Practitioner, Doula, Mother
San Francisco, CA

The first time I became consciously aware of the Great Mother was as a young child on my grandparents' farm. Every spring at lambing time, my grandmother would assist the birthing animals. She allowed me to help, and it was at her side that I first experienced the power of the Great Mother. At first, I thought it was my grandmother who had the power, but she explained it was the "womanly power of God" and the power of the land working through her to help the animals give birth.

When I am connected to the Great Mother, the breadth and depth of her power is present for me and for my clients. By tapping into her power, healing is more possible for my clients, and I am also held by that power. I am able to maintain and support myself when I am connected to her. By working with her power rather than my own, I do not risk becoming burned out.

Working with the Great Mother has brought me a deeper sense of belonging and connection. My life is guided by her wisdom. Coming into greater alignment with the Great Mother has brought me greater clarity, healing, deeper relationships, and greater freedom to create the life I came here to lead.

Healing done within the framework of Depth Hypnosis is about restoring the connection to the deeper self. This involves healing our connection to our source. When I work with a woman who is preparing for birth, my intention is to provide her with a direct connection to the Great Mother. I help her deepen that connection so that she can draw upon that connection during labor. If I am also her birth doula, I work in the birth to remind her of that connection during the labor process. If she is unable to hold her connection to the Great Mother, I hold it for her. I also work with the Great Mother with postpartum women to heal any trauma that might have occurred during the birth.

TRANSFORMATION

I had the opportunity to work with a very strong Latina woman, Maria, who was carrying a great deal of trauma from having a very difficult and painful life. She was birthing her second child and had previously had a traumatic experience with her first child's birth. She had experienced a great deal of violence and pain in her life, including sexual abuse. She was a single mother with very limited resources and was living in a dangerous neighborhood.

Her relationship with her mother was strained and almost nonexistent due the violence she had experienced in that relationship. She had survived and adapted to these difficulties by becoming tough and hard. When I arrived for my first prenatal visit at her home, I was put through a series of tests to determine whether I was worthy to work with her. Looking back now at that first meeting, I smile; but at the time, I was nervous and afraid.

On the surface, we could not be more different. We came from completely different backgrounds. I wondered, "What do I have to offer her that she could accept?" I tried to create a common ground through womanhood and motherhood. Finally, I acknowledged our differences and asked for her trust and permission to work with her. She accepted my request, and we began our journey together.

In our session work, it became clear that the hard, protective shell Maria adopted had caused problems in her first birth. She had been unable to relax and trust her birth attendants or her body. This resulted in a long and painful birth with a very stressed baby. Underneath her toughness, she was terrified of giving birth again. She was a woman who did not trust support. Also, because of her troubled relationship with her mother, she did not trust other women at all.

It took many sessions, but, eventually, I was able to work with guided meditations to connect her with the power of the Great Mother. The Great Mother came in a very gentle and nurturing form. Maria connected deeply to the Great Mother through movement and dance. We stayed focused on her allowing for support and gentleness. A bit of trust was also developing between the two of us, yet she remained very fearful of the upcoming birth. We kept working.

When the baby was ready to be born, Maria called me and I went to her side. She was in a great deal of distress, and I kept reminding her of the dance of the Great Mother.

She was still trying to be tough and to muscle through. We were at a birthing center. At one point, she asked her midwife to leave. I stayed with her as she shook and broke down. I was deeply connected with the Great Mother, and she helped me understand that the tough shell was breaking apart.

Shortly after this shaking, Maria went into transition. She wanted me to sit behind her and hold her body as she labored and pushed her baby out. I remember the power of the Great Mother pouring through my body into Maria. I was a conduit for the Great Mother to move into her body. With every contraction, I focused that power for Maria, and she took it in deeply and used it.

When the baby began to crown, she started to scream and disassociate. She started yelling for the birth to stop and she demanded that the midwife take the baby out. She was being triggered by the trauma of her sexual abuse and the trauma of her previous birth.

I was listening to the Great Mother. As she instructed, I asked Maria to remember the dance of the Great Mother and to move that way. I reminded her that she was safe and could do the work of pushing her baby out.

With me still seated behind her, she began to ease into a different movement and relax a bit. The baby was born shortly thereafter.

It was a difficult and beautiful birth that would have looked very different without both of our connections to the power of the Great Mother.

At her postpartum visit, Maria told me that this birth was the most powerful moment of her life. We were working on an art project with her placenta, and she recounted the entire trauma in her life in a very open way. I remember the look on her face when she said the birth had changed all that, and she knew she would be okay.

She went back to school and is now a teacher. She is raising her children on her own and giving them a stable life. I recently spoke with her, and she shared her dream with me of becoming a midwife herself. I attribute all of these gifts to the love and nurturance of the Great Mother's presence at her birth.

CONCLUSION

These stories offer a window into the initiation of birth. They demonstrate the benefit of being empowered during birth and a way of connecting to power for this purpose. They also illustrate the change that accompanies initiation and the positive, long lasting benefits that this change brings to the lives of women who are empowered in this way. To recognize the Great Mother is to give a name to something that is often nameless, yet is always there. By doing so, we invite the discussion of this power into the contemporary dialogue around birth. It is not meant to codify something, just to point to it. Acknowledging this power offers women a place of focus and an invitation to step into their own power with clarity and conviction.

The initiation of birth is different for every woman, just as the experience of giving birth is different. Yet giving birth is part of our lineage as women. It is my hope that bringing the power of giving birth into focus, through the relationship to the Great Mother, will help empower women in the birth process and in their lives.

APPENDIX: GREAT MOTHER MEDITATION

You find yourself getting comfortable. Noticing all of the places that the surface under you meets the different parts of your body. And as you feel yourself supported in this way, notice where your breath is.

Notice all of the places where your breath meets the different parts of your body. Notice where your breath goes as you breathe in and where your breath goes as you breathe out.

Now notice how your breath when you inhale and your breath when you exhale is like a bridge between your outer world and your inner world. With each breath notice how you draw more and more closely in to your inner world.

We are taking a journey into that place within you where everything that you have ever known or felt or sensed or imagined is recorded. And we are taking a journey to this place within you to connect with the power of the Great Mother. This may be sensed in a variety of ways. You may hear it, you may see it, you may feel it, you may smell it, or you may just be aware of it through your sixth sense.

Open to this idea in whatever way feels best to you. You may experience this part of yourself as an image, a beautiful light, a sound, as a teacher in human or plant or animal form, as an angelic or mythical being, or some other form that has special significance to you.

But for now, just return to your breath. And as you do, just sense or feel or imagine that there is relaxation all around you. Now on your next breath, draw this sense of relaxation into your head and face, letting all of the muscles around your eyes and jaw release any tension that you might be carrying. Notice your neck and throat and feel that relaxation flow down into your shoulders and arms and hands. Feel your fingertips as the relaxing feeling reaches them. They may tingle a little bit.

Now allow this feeling of relaxation to flow down into your chest and belly. Just notice how your organs of digestion, respiration, reproduction, and elimination are bathed in this relaxation. Just feeling that same relaxation flow down into your hips, your knees, down into your ankles and into your feet. You may feel your toes tingling a bit as that relaxation reaches all the way down into the tips.

Now on your next breath try to sense or feel or imagine that this relaxation has created a star or a sun or a ball of warm light at the base of your skull. And can you sense or feel or imagine that it is radiating throughout your mind, harmonizing your brain waves and relaxing your mind. And just notice how as your mind relaxes, your body relaxes, and as your body relaxes, your mind relaxes even more. Allow yourself to sense the connection between your mind and your body as this relaxation flows down your spine vertebra by vertebra.

Now just feel this relaxation flow all the way down the back of your body. You may even feel that you are so filled with this relaxation that it is coming out of the pores of your body and surrounding you in a cocoon or cloud of soothing gentle energy.

And as you find yourself relaxed in this way, try to sense or feel or imagine that there is a staircase here before you. This staircase leads you closer to that place within you where you will make a connection with the power of the Great Mother. Now just allow yourself, as I count from ten to one, to travel along this staircase knowing that when I reach the number one you will be in that place where you will make this connection with the power of the Great Mother.

10 – Feeling your feet on the stair.

9 – Feeling your hand on the guardrail, knowing that you have complete control over this process.

8 – Knowing that if anything should become overwhelming for any reason, you can count yourself out from one to 10.

7 – *Knowing that you can go quite deeply because of all of the work you have already done.*

6 – *Knowing that you can now let all of your inner senses open widely.*

5 – *Allowing your inner sense of taste, touch, smell, sight, hearing, and especially that sixth sense to open widely.*

4 – *And now bringing all of your inner senses and focusing them on a place, perhaps in nature, where you have felt comfortable and at peace.*

3 – *Knowing that you can let your conscious mind take a well-deserved rest as you focus on this place where you feel comfortable and at peace.*

2 – *Knowing that you can trust the impressions that you are receiving as you focus on this place where you feel comfortable and at peace.*

1 – *As you get to the end of the staircase, allow yourself to step out into this place.*

Take a deep breath. Notice the quality of the light. Listen for any sounds. Notice if there is a wind on your cheek. You may notice for the first time in a long time how much this place is a part of you and how much you are a part of this place. Just feel that connection.

And then, even though it is so relaxing to be here again, I wonder if you can sense or feel or imagine that there is a path, a very inviting path, leading away from this place and leading to the place where you will make the connection with the power of the Great Mother.

Now I am going to count from one to four. When I reach the number four you will find yourself in the presence, or very close to being in the presence, of this part of yourself that you may perceive as a light, or sound, or animal, or teacher in human or plant form, or that angel, or mythic being, or some other form that has significance for you.

1 – *You find your feet on the path. Notice what the path is made of.*

2 – Knowing that you will be able to talk to me loudly and clearly to describe your experience.

3 – Knowing that you can trust the impressions that you are receiving and knowing that your conscious mind can take a well-deserved rest.

4 – Now finding yourself in the presence or very close to the presence of the power of the Great Mother.

And now that you are feeling the depth of your connection to this place, can you look around and sense or feel or imagine a presence, knowing that this presence is the power of the Great Mother. You may perceive this presence as a light or sound or animal or teacher in human or plant form or that angel or mythic being -- anything that has significance for you. And ask the power of the Great Mother, "Would you be willing to guide me and protect me and those I serve?"

You may receive this answer as a spoken or telepathic communication, or a change in the environment, or an action on the part of the power of the Great Mother, or a knowing. Just letting yourself rest in this answer, knowing that more insights and understandings about the nature of this connection will come in the days ahead.

But for now, with each number I count, make your connection with the power of the Great Mother stronger and deeper and wider.

1 – You feel the connection with the power of the Great Mother deeply.

2 – You are back on the staircase taking the same path to where you began.

3 – With each step you are moving closer to the surface.

4 – With each step the connection is becoming more pronounced.

5 – You are halfway back along the staircase.

6 – You are beginning to feel the chair under you.

7 – You may want to stretch a bit.

8 – You are almost at the end of the staircase.

9 – Taking all the time you need, feel yourself coming back into the room.

10 – You reach the end of the staircase and are fully back in the room.

BIBLIOGRAPHY

Block, Jennifer. *Pushed: The Painful Truth About Childbirth and Modern Maternity Care*. Cambridge, MA: Da Capo Press, 2007.

Campbell, Joseph. *The Hero with a Thousand Faces*. 3rd ed. Novato, CA: New World Library, 2008.

Ehrenreich, Barbara and Deirdre English. *Witches, Midwives, & Nurses: A History of Women Healers*. New York: Feminist Press, 1973.

Epstein, Abby, director. *The Business of Being Born*. DVD. Burbank, CA: New Line Home Entertainment, 2008.

Gaskin, Ina May. *Ina May's Guide to Childbirth*. New York: Bantam Books, 2003.

Grof, Stanislav. *Beyond the Brain: Birth, Death and Transcendence in Psychotherapy*. Albany: State University of New York Press, 1985.

Jones, Amy Cox. *The Way of the Peaceful Birther*. Springbrook, WI: Salt of the Earth Press, 2010.

Kinsley, David R. *Hindu Goddesses: Visions of the Divine Feminine in the Hindu Religious Tradition*. Berkeley: University of California Press, 1988.

Lucas, Winafred Blake. *Regression Therapy: a Handbook for Professionals*. Crest Park, CA: Deep Forest Press, 1993.

Mariscotti de Gorlitz, Ana Maria. *Pachamama Santa Tierra: Estudia de la Religion Autoctona en los Andes Centro-meridionales*. Berlin: Mann, 1978.

Reed, Ellen Cannon. *Circle of Isis: Ancient Egyptian Magic for Modern Witches*. Franklin Lakes, NJ: Career Press, 2002.

Rigoglioso, Marguerite. *Virgin Mother Goddesses of Antiquity*. New York: Palgrave Macmillan, 2010.

Sogyal Rinpoche. *The Tibetan Book of Living and Dying*. Edited by Patrick Gaffney and Andrew Harvey. San Francisco: HarperCollins, 1994.

Wertz, Richard W. and Dorothy C. Wertz. *Lying-In: A History of Childbirth in America.* expanded ed. New Haven: Yale University Press, 1989.

Williams, E. Leslie. *Spirit Tree: Origins of Cosmology in Shintô Ritual at Hakozaki.* Lanham, MD: University Press of America, 2007.

Waters, Frank. *Book of the Hopi.* New York: Penguin Books, 1977.

Willson, Martin. *In Praise of Tara: Songs to the Saviouress.* Boston: Wisdom Publications: 1996.

Made in the USA
Lexington, KY
09 May 2014